The Red Light Series:
Fumble

Kiana Martenique

Halo
PUBLISHING
INTERNATIONAL

ISBN: 978-1-63765-253-4
LCCN: 2022910461

Halo Publishing International, LLC
www.halopublishing.com

Printed and bound in the United States of America

This book is dedicated to my dad. He always encouraged me and Loved to read my new writings. He was Excited when both Eligible Receivers and Pass Interference were released. I know he heard the Words "Well done, thou good and faithful servant" (Matthew 25:21). Dad. The Man. The Myth. The Legend. Although he is not here for this release of Fumble, I know.he is looking down on us and will Always be with us in spirit!

Contents

Introduction

Remember that we are all eligible to receive the promises God has for us! You may see Scriptures repeated in this book, or even phrases such as "greater is coming," but it is with good reason. Sometimes we need repetition. That helps us get it into our spirit. Helps encourage and push us through to do what God's Word needs us to do in that moment. Helps even to correct us.

The Father knows all, hears all, and sees all. He knows what we are going to do before we do it. But the beautiful thing is He never holds sin against us. He wants us to repent, to turn to Him, so we can be ready to receive the promise.

Chapter 1

A New Creature

Therefore if any man be in Christ, he is a new creature: old things are passed away; behold, all things are become new.
—*2 Corinthians 5:17*

I am reminded of an album title, *Perfectly Imperfect*, by one of my favorite singers, Elle Varner. We are definitely not perfect people, but we are made perfect in God. Remember that God loves you, every part of you. He knows what makes you tick. He knows you better than anyone, better than you know yourself. And if you have been broken by things that have happened in your life, know that God desires to give you beauty for your ashes. No matter what may have happened in your life, better is coming!

You can know who you are, but it's more important to know who you are in Christ.

Meditate on this Scripture:

Therefore, my beloved brethren, be ye steadfast, unmovable, always abounding in the work of the Lord, forasmuch as ye know that your labor is not in vain in the Lord.

—1 Corinthians 15:58

My Testimony

I will definitely say this—I have been a loner many years. If I had any friends, there were maybe a few, or one, with the other two really being associates. That has given me a lot of alone time—LOL. Spending a lot of time by yourself causes you to learn who you really are. You can go to a movie or get something to eat by yourself, even hang out with just you. I remember the first time I went to a movie by myself; I was fifteen. My friend was afraid of snakes, so that meant I had to see *Anaconda* alone—LOL. Ever since then, I have enjoyed seeing a movie on my own.

The older I got, the more I began to understand that I would be doing things on my own quite often. Because I was saved, my peers did not want to do the things I liked...and I did not want to party, drink, etc., with them. So you know I definitely was not popular in college—LOL. But my identity in Christ caused me to not want to partake of certain things. I was often called a goody-goody, or told that I thought I was "all that," from my teens through my twenties.

But I was neither of those things. I was just a young lady who knew right from wrong about certain things, according to my faith in God, according to what I knew was in His Word. Even when I was pressured by peers, I could not do certain things because I just felt out of place or weird about it. I will share more in chapter three.

I thank God for bringing me through all that He has and for teaching me from a young age who I am in Him. I thank Him for His correction and direction. I thank Him for His encouragement during those times I have felt lonely, for His reminder that I am not alone.

Remember that you are never alone! You may feel different or that you don't belong, but there is no person on Earth who can be who you are. Hang in there! You are special; you are you!

A Prayer

Thank you, Heavenly Father, for teaching me the things of You and showing me who I am in You. I want to know You more and more each day. I thank You and ask that my steps be ordered in Your Word, and I thank You for loving me unconditionally. Thank you, God, for showing me what I don't know, for guiding me, and for directing me in the way I should go. In Jesus's name, amen.

Scriptures about Walking with God

For we are his workmanship, created in Christ Jesus unto good works, which God hath ordained that we should walk in them.

—Ephesians 2:10

That ye might walk worthy of the Lord unto all pleasing, being fruitful in every good work, and increasing in the knowledge of God; strengthened with all might, according to his glorious power, unto all patience and longsuffering with joyfulness.

—Colossians 1:10–11

Therefore thou shalt keep the commandments of the Lord thy God, to walk in his ways, and to fear him.

—Deuteronomy 8:6

Let us walk honestly, as in the day; not in rioting and drunkenness, not in chambering and wantonness, not in strife and envying.

—Romans 13:13

This I say then, Walk in the Spirit and ye shall not fulfil the lust of the flesh.

—Galatians 5:16

Let us draw near with a true heart in full assurance of faith, having our hearts sprinkled from an evil conscience, and our bodies washed with pure water.

—Hebrews 10:22

Looking unto Jesus the author and finisher of our faith; who for the joy that was set before him endured the cross, despising the shame, and is set down at the right hand of the throne of God.

—Hebrews 12:2

And he answering said, Thou shalt love the Lord thy God with all thy heart, and with all thy soul, and with all thy strength, and with all thy mind; and thy neighbor as thyself.

—Luke 10:27

Being confident of this very thing, that he which hath begun a good work in you will perform it until the day of Jesus Christ.

—Philippians 1:6

Take the next two pages for your own personal study and devotional.

Personal Study and Devotional

Chapter 1

Personal Study and Devotional

Chapter 1

Chapter 2

In Possession

Every good gift and every perfect gift is from above, and cometh down from the Father of lights, with whom is no variableness, neither shadow of turning.

—James 1:17

So, you are an eligible receiver. You are a new creature when you give your life to Jesus Christ. You have possession of the ball!

This football represents a "good" and "perfect gift," just as the Word says in James 1:17. It can be anything you have ever hoped for or dreamed about. Have no fear! Sometimes it may seem as if the dream is bigger than you, but, remember, we serve a great God who does BIG things for us all. He is preparing us, setting us up for success.

So now the question comes—what do you do next? Well, in a football game, we know what usually comes next—LOL. A play is executed—a player may even run the ball and make a touchdown! That is the ultimate goal, to take what God has given and make it successful, complete it, to honor Him with it...to score!

What God has for you is for you. You have possession of the ball! :-)

Meditate on this Scripture:

The Blessing of the Lord, it maketh rich, and he addeth no sorrow with it.

—*Proverbs 10:22*

My Testimony

Well, if I could write down how many times I have been in possession of the ball... To name a few, God gave me the opportunity to go to college and get a degree. I am blessed with a good job. I own my own car. I am debt-free. There are so many other things I could mention if I just sat to think of them all. God has been so good to me, even when I did not deserve it—even when I wanted more things than He wanted for me.

A Prayer

I thank You, God, for being better to me than anyone could ever be. I thank You for giving me possession of the ball. I know that Your ways are not my ways, and Your thoughts are not my thoughts, Lord, as you say in Your Word. I thank You for all that You have blessed me with and all

You are going to bless me with. You do BIG things, God! You are awesome! In Jesus's name, I pray. Amen.

Scriptures about Being in Possession of God's Blessing

Grant thee according to thine own heart, and fulfil all thy counsel.

—Psalms 20:4

The Lord Bless thee, and keep thee: The Lord make his face shine upon thee, and be gracious unto thee: The Lord lift up his countenance upon thee, and give thee peace.

—Numbers 6:24–26

Commit thy works unto the Lord, and thy thoughts shall be established.

—Proverbs 16:3

For I know the thoughts that I think toward you, saith the Lord, thoughts of peace, and not of evil, to give you an expected end.

—Jeremiah 29:11

O taste and see that the Lord is good: blessed is the man that trusteth in him.

—Psalms 34:8

Bring ye all the tithes into the storehouse, that there may be meat in mine house, and prove me now herewith, saith the Lord of hosts, if I will not open you the windows of heaven, and pour you out a blessing, that there shall not be room enough to receive it.

—*Malachi 3:10*

Take the next two pages for your own personal study and devotional.

Personal Study and Devotional

Chapter 2

Personal Study and Devotional

Chapter 2

Chapter 3

I Fumbled Your Heart

Therefore to him that knoweth to do good,
and doeth [it] not, to him it is sin.

—*James 4:17*

Let's talk about sin, as mentioned in James 4:17. When God gives us an opportunity or blesses us with something, it is a sin when we fumble the ball, when we waste it. We all are guilty of this for different reasons. You may have thought you could pay for what you charged on credit, but then ended up laid off from your job and unable to make the payments, which sent you further into debt. You may have thought you could have a better relationship with someone, but that person ended up treating you very badly. You may have thought you had time to go back to school, but your procrastination caused you to lose grant money or a scholarship. These are all examples of when we fumble the ball.

It is important to get your head back into the game after a fumble. Never allow yourself to be beat up by guilt. That is always the number one tactic the enemy uses against God's children. He wants to make you feel bad, and his biggest hope is that you will become depressed. I mentioned in *Eligible Receivers* and *Pass Interference* how I went through this.

God has already forgiven you! Remember that. He loves you. Now is the time to speak the Word over your situation because that is your sword with which to fight. Speak life over your situation. The Father knows how to turn things around for you!

Remember that sin creates a barrier to being in possession of your blessing. It causes you to fumble the ball. Confess your sin to the Lord, and He will forgive you!

Meditate on this Scripture:

> *If my people, which are called by my name, shall humble themselves, and pray, and seek my face, and turn from their wicked ways; then will I hear from heaven, and I will forgive their sin, and will heal their land.*

> —*2 Chronicles 7:14*

My Testimony

When writing this chapter, I thought of some of the lyrics and chorus from "Fumble" by Trey Songz. In this song, he is talking about a relationship with another person, but I can relate it to my relationship with the Lord. I love to flip songs, as many of you know, so here we go!

In terms of dating relationships, I often held on to my past. I would not let go of something older, more familiar, even if it was not the best relationship for me. In a part of the song, Trey is pleading with his lady, telling her that he loves her, that he knows he really messed up, and that he will give her his all if she will forgive him.

I have done this with the Lord, even when I went into debt in my late twenties and filed bankruptcy. Whatever I did that was wrong, I felt bad—just as Trey feels bad in that song—and I wanted God to know that was really sorry. I wanted to start over, to be better. I learned my lesson.

I understand, to this very day, that you must release the guilt. That's how you move forward. Die to yourself daily. As it says in Luke 9:23, "And he said to them all, If any man will come after me, let him deny himself, and take up his cross daily, and follow me."

Parts of another song that I will reference here is "Bad Habits" by Usher. Even the title is self-explanatory. Cheating will put a good relationship in jeopardy. Having a desire for things that you shouldn't or for someone whom you shouldn't can jeopardize your future. What I like in this song by Usher is that he is saying that God knows his heart, that he wants to do the right thing, and that he wants to be able to love this girl. But he always ends up giving into his flesh and being with other women.

How many times have we done something wrong and asked God to forgive us? Right? Sometimes you can be your own worst enemy. You can be the reason why you have not received a blessing from God. You can be the reason why you aren't moving in the direction God has chosen for you, and that is ALWAYS FORWARD. God moves you forward. He elevates you. He takes you to higher heights!

You can't keep going back to an ex if you want to be blessed with God's best for you! You can't cheat in your relationship! You can't cheat on your wife or husband! You can't have sex before marriage! You can't keep masturbating or watching porn if you want God's best for you! You can't keep coveting what other people have if you want God's best for you! And, basically, you can't continue to sin if you want to be blessed!

I am not judging; I'm just keeping it very real. To use the title of the previous book in the series, in order to make a point here, you are causing there to be a pass interference when you do any of these things. You are causing a delay of your blessing!

You want to receive that pass from God. He has been trying to pass you such a great blessing, and you cannot receive your wife or your husband into your life until you let everything else go! Make space. Make room. When you let go of what God no longer wants you to have—or maybe never wanted you to have in the first place—you make room for your blessings to come!

If it's something you feel you cannot do, you need deliverance. That is something God can do for you—deliver you from whatever or whomever it is. Just call on Him! Call on Jesus! He is more than able to remove that desire from you!

It took me many years, but I surrendered my dating life totally to God. Before that, I went back to my ex because he was familiar. I compromised my faith to be with him. I also dated other guys, with whom I was unequally yoked, just because I was lonely. I did not want to wait to have a relationship with someone to whom I would be equally yoked. I did that for nine years.

Once I surrendered my dating life totally to God at age thirty-four, I stopped dating. I haven't dated for six years because I know that God has been calling me to be a wife to a specific someone in His perfect timing. It's ALL about God's will and His way for my life—not mine! As it should be for you! :-)

A Prayer

Father, God, I thank You for loving me unconditionally. You have always looked beyond my faults and seen my needs. There is no one like You or greater than You! Thank You for forgiving me anything I have done wrong and for showing me the right way to go. Help me to do what is pleasing in Your sight because I want to please You and be in right standing with You. I thank You for Your wisdom, Your grace, and Your mercy. In Jesus's name, amen.

Scriptures for When You Fumble the Ball

And they that are Christ's have crucified the flesh with the affections and lusts.

—*Galatians 5:24*

Verily, verily, I say unto you, Except a corn of wheat fall into the ground and die, it abideth alone: but if it die, it bringeth forth much fruit.

—*John 12:24*

For me to live [is] Christ, and to die [is] gain.

—*Philippians 1:21*

—*Romans 8*

In whom we have redemption through his blood the forgiveness of sins, according to the riches of his grace.

—*Ephesians 1:7*

How much more shall the blood of Christ, who through the eternal Spirit offered himself without spot to God, purge your conscience from dead works to serve the living God?

—*Hebrews 9:14*

Submit yourselves therefore to God. Resist the devil, and he will flee from you.

—*James 4:7*

The righteous cry, and the LORD heareth, and delivereth them out of all their troubles.

—*Psalms 34:17*

Stand fast therefore in the liberty wherewith Christ hath made us free, and be not entangled again with the yoke of bondage.

—*Galatians 5:1*

And when he had called unto him his twelve disciples, he gave them power against unclean spirits, to cast them out, and to heal all manner of sickness and all manner of disease.

—*Matthew 10:1*

The Lord knoweth how to deliver the godly out of temptations.

—*2 Peter 2:9*

Be pleased, O LORD, to deliver me: O LORD, make haste to help me.

—*Psalms 40:13*

Put on the whole armour of God, that ye may be able to stand against the wiles of the devil.

—*Ephesians 6:11*

Take the next two pages for your own personal study and devotional.

Personal Study and Devotional

Chapter 3

Personal Study and Devotional

Chapter 3

Chapter 4

A Turnover

And Moses commanded the children of Israel according to the word of the LORD, saying, The tribe of the sons of Joseph hath said well.

This is the thing which the Lord doth command concerning the daughters of Zelophehad, saying, Let them marry to whom they think best; only to the family of the tribe of their father shall they marry.

So shall not the inheritance of the children of Israel remove from tribe to tribe: for every one of the children of Israel shall keep himself to the inheritance of the tribe of his fathers.

And every daughter, that possesseth an inheritance in any tribe of the children of Israel shall be wife unto one of the family of the tribe of her father, that the children of Israel may enjoy every man the inheritance of his fathers.

Neither shall the inheritance remove from one tribe to another tribe; but every one of the tribes of the children of Israel shall keep himself to his own inheritance.

—*Numbers 36:5–9*

I decided to use the children of Israel to reference promise. For a time, they went against God; they did the wrong things. But in the end, they reached the Promised Land. I am remembering the phrase "a hard head makes a soft behind"—LOL. That could be said about many of us.

When you are in possession of the ball, remember you are holding a precious promise from God. You must be careful with it; if not, you are running the risk of someone coming along and taking possession of what belongs to you. Never let go of the ball, the promise. Don't take the promise for granted. Don't get lazy. Stay focused on the ball. You don't want to see your promises, your hopes, and your dreams—all that you have prayed for—in the hands of someone else.

Remember, with a divine will, God has ordained what your life is to be. A great example is whom you marry. For some people, God chooses a spouse. They may be in ministry together or performing whatever purpose God has intended for them to be joined and working on together. Sometimes all God requires us to do is hold on to the ball, the promise. To believe. To have faith while holding on. "Faith without works is dead," according to James

2:20. Faith with works will help you take that ball on in for a touchdown!

When you are in possession of the ball, the promise, you must be careful with it. You don't want to see your promise, your hopes and dreams, what you have prayed for, in the hands of someone else.

Meditate on this Scripture:

> *And let us not be weary in well doing: for in due season we shall reap, if we faint not.*

> —*Galatians 6:9*

My Testimony

Many people often give up on holding on to the promise because they get discouraged. This is also the number one tactic the enemy uses to get people to want to take their own lives, to commit suicide.

I remember feeling that way. The only reason I did not commit suicide was because I was too scared to do it. Sometimes God uses fear in a good way. I wanted to give up on life, on the promise I was told about in more than one prophecy. I would wait and wait, and years would pass by, and nothing would happen. I was so unhappy.

I had to learn to accept that everything happens in God's timing. It's not Kiana's will, but God's will. When.

Where. How. Just keep holding on until the day and time comes when God says, "Now!"

If the enemy can depress someone, discourage someone, distract someone from believing in the promise God has for them, he will do it! Never—I repeat, never—lose sight of God's promise for you. Never lose sight of the ball.

When it comes to God's divine will, know that if another person has possession of the ball, it is only temporary. What God has for you is for you! Continue doing what you know you should do. Be "in the game," so to speak. When you do that, God steps in and does what He must to make things right. In His timing, things will be the way He always meant for them to be!

A Prayer

Thank You, God, for loving me so much that You took the time to create special blessings just for me! Thank You for loving me unconditionally and completely. Show me, Father, God, how to hold on to the promise You have for me in my life. Give me people to encourage my spirit and uplift me. Show me how to encourage and uplift myself. I thank You, God, and know that in Your timing, You will exceedingly and abundantly provide more than I could ever ask for or think possible! In Jesus's name, amen.

Scriptures to Help You Hold On to Your Promise

Fear thou not; for I am with thee: be not dismayed;
for I am thy God: I will strengthen thee; yea, I will
help thee; yea, I will uphold thee with the right hand of
my righteousness.

—Isaiah 41:10

And David was greatly distressed; for the people spake
of stoning him, because the soul of all the people was
grieved, every man for his sons and his for his daugh-
ters: but David encouraged himself in the LORD
his God.

—1 Samuel 30:6

Thou wilt shew me the path of life: in thy presence
is fullness of joy; at thy right hand there are plea-
sures forevermore.

—Psalms 16:11

Wherefore seeing we also are compassed about with
so great a cloud of witnesses, let us lay aside every
weight, and the sin which doth so easily beset us, and
let us run with patience the race that is set before us,
2 Looking unto Jesus, the author and finisher of our
faith; who for the joy that was set before him endured
the cross, despising the shame, and is set down at the
right hand of the throne of God.

—Hebrews 12:1–2

Scriptures on What to Do if There Has Been a Turnover

Even so faith, if it hath not works, is dead, being alone.

—James 2:17

As an earring of gold, and an ornament of fine gold, so is a wise reprover upon an obedient ear.

—Proverbs 25:12

Be careful for nothing; but in everything by prayer and supplication with thanksgiving let your requests be made known unto God. And the peace of God, which passeth all understanding shall keep your hearts and minds through Christ Jesus.

—Philippians 4:6–7

Call unto me, and I will answer thee, and show thee great and mighty things, which thou knowest not.

—Jeremiah 33:3

Trust in the Lord with all thine heart; and lean not unto thine own understanding. 6 In all thy ways acknowledge him, and he shall direct thy paths.

—Proverbs 3:5–6

Take the next two pages for your own personal study and devotional.

Personal Study and Devotional

Chapter 4

Personal Study and Devotional

Chapter 4

Chapter 5

Halftime

I will lift up mine eyes unto the hills, from whence cometh my help.

My help cometh from the LORD, which made heaven and earth.

He will not suffer thy foot to be moved: he that keepeth thee will not slumber.

Behold, he that keepeth Israel shall neither slumber nor sleep.

The LORD is thy keeper: the LORD is thy shade upon thy right hand.

The sun shall not smite thee by day, nor the moon by night.

The LORD shall preserve thee from all evil: he shall preserve thy soul.

The LORD shall preserve thy going out and thy coming in from this time forth, and even for evermore.

—*Psalms 121*

Now you have gotten to the point where you have experienced a fumble in the game, or even a turnover. You have read the Scriptures in the last chapter on what to do if there has been a turnover. You realize that, no matter what has happened in the game, you must remain focused. You can't allow the enemy to take you down. You can't allow him to crush your spirit. Remember, he wants to crush your spirit so that he can defeat you.

This is halftime. It is time to regroup, to refresh. Spend time with the Father. Sing to Him. Worship Him. Praise Him. Turn your attention to the things not of this world, but of Him. According to Psalms 121, our "help cometh from the Lord!" This reminds us that we can't do everything by ourselves. When the game gets hard, you have to turn to Him and say, "Father, help me! I'm sinking deep. I am drowning in this, and I need Your help! Only You can help me. Only You can turn this around for me."

God is the head coach. He's right there with you, not only during halftime in the game, but throughout your entire life. He will "never leave thee, nor forsake thee," according to Hebrews 13:5! Think of it this way—He has a book full of plays just for you. If you execute those plays, you will experience all that He wants for you in this life.

Our Father knows the moves you are going to make before you make them. All He asks is that you stay under His shelter, so that no one and nothing can come between you and His love for you.

So, get some Gatorade—LOL—or any refreshing drink of your choice, and make sure your armor is on so that you can be prepared for round two, the second half of the game.

Here is some encouragement for you: If you have had a tough life, even early on, God desires to give you "beauty for ashes," according to Isaiah 61:1–3. Greater things are coming! It may be today, next week, or even in the next months. Just keep God in your life, and never let Him go. He is always there with you!

Get pumped up! Sometimes you have to pump yourself up. You are one step closer to a win, to getting what God wants you to have!

This is halftime. It is when we get to spend time with our Heavenly Father, regroup, and refresh…and get direction on what to do next in the game.

Meditate on this Scripture:

I can do all things through Christ which strengtheneth me.

—Philippians 4:13

My Testimony

I know what it is to feel defeated, to feel as if you just want to give up. There have been many times when I have been so low that I have cried; I remember doing so one New Year's Eve and even at Christmas. Why? Because I had no friends. Because the guy I had been dating and thought I would marry had slept with his ex. Because I did not fit in at my job. Because I did not fit in at church. There are so many becauses I could add here. But I won't. Because they don't matter!

Yes, I have felt sad. Yes, things have happened to bring me down, but I had to take my hurt to God and tell Him all about everything. As much as I wanted and needed to. I had to spend time with Him. Loving Him, even when my energy was low from a broken spirit. He loved me right back, every time!

In those quiet moments I spent talking to God, sometimes He would do sweet things to lift my spirit, such as play a favorite song when I turned on the radio, or show me see something that made me laugh, or even see to it that I got free food when I went to my favorite restaurant.

After He cheered me up, I would dust myself off, wipe my tears, and say, "What should I do next, God?" If He didn't answer right away, I would just find positive things to do and continue to talk to Him and sing to Him. Eventually, I would hear a timely Word to help me, or I would be blessed by someone whom God had sent with a gift or an act of sharing. God has always answered in one way or another. He always shows up on time!

A Prayer

I thank You, Father, God, for Your love, Your peace that surpasses all understanding, and Your joy! I know that You can handle any situation. You can do anything but fail! I thank You for continuing to encourage me and for loving me. No one knows me better than You do, and I know You have great things in store for me. Thank You for being my strength, Lord, and for giving me the strength to do what I need to do to receive all the things You have for me! In Jesus's name, I pray. Amen.

Scriptures to Help You Regroup and Refresh

These things I have spoken unto you, that in me ye might have peace. In the world ye shall have tribulation: but be of good cheer; I have overcome the world.

—John 16:33

Thou wilt keep [him] in perfect peace, [whose] mind [is] stayed [on thee]: because he trusteth in thee.

—Isaiah 26:3

And the God of peace shall bruise Satan under your feet shortly. The grace of our Lord Jesus Christ [be] with you. Amen.

—Romans 16:10

Therefore being justified by faith, we have peace with God through our Lord Jesus Christ.

—*Romans 5:1*

For his anger endureth but for a moment; in his favor is life: weeping may endure for a night, but joy cometh in the morning.

—*Psalms 30:5*

And he arose, and rebuked the wind, and said unto the sea, Peace, be still. And the wind ceased, and there was a great calm.

—*Mark 4:39*

Take the next two pages for your own personal study and devotional.

Personal Study and Devotional

Chapter 5

Personal Study and Devotional

Chapter 5

Chapter 6

Second Half

And let us not be weary in well doing: for in
due season we shall reap, if we faint not.

—Galatians 6:9

You've just come out of halftime. You are refreshed. You have a Word from the Lord. You have direction. You have a peace that "passeth all understanding," according to Philippians 4:7. You are suited in the armor of God. Your war clothes are on. Ready for victory? Now it's game time!

Ecclesiastes 9:11 says, "I returned, and saw under the sun, that the race is not to the swift, nor the battle to the strong, neither yet bread to the wise, nor yet riches to men of understanding, nor yet favour to men of skill; but time and chance happeneth to them all."

This Scripture is what you must remember! No matter what you have gone through, persevere. Never doubt. You are an eligible receiver! You were born to win! What God has for you will always be there for you! Make no mistake about it. Get in position. Your turn is coming to take that ball down the field. You are headed for a touchdown! At the right place and time, whatever God has promised you will come to pass. It is oftentimes when you least expect it!

God is right there with each of us, in the trenches and helping us every day. He is always setting us up to win! When you get your wins, record them as a reminder to yourself of what God has done for you. When you remember what He has done for you, you recall what He is capable of doing. There is nothing He can't do! It is also a reminder that He does great things, above and beyond all that we ask or think possible!

Get in position. It is your time to win!

Meditate on this Scripture:

Therefore, my beloved brethren, be ye steadfast, unmovable, always abounding in the work of the Lord, forasmuch as ye know that your labour is not in vain in the Lord.

—*1 Corinthians 15:58*

My Testimony

I love music, as all the readers of my books and blog know. That is one thing that God uses for me in times when my spirit needs a pick-me-up. I am reminded of a song sung by Men of Standard; it is called "In Your Will." It's a very simple song that you can repeat over and over. It gets into your spirit. It does that for me. It's something to push you forward and cheer you on...because greater things are coming to you! And as I mentioned before, it's your time to win!

A Prayer

Heavenly Father, I thank You for all that You have done for me, and all that You are about to do for me. You do all things well! You are great! You are strong! You are mighty! You are good! You are omnipotent, omnipresent, and omniscient! Help me to stay in position, God, to stay in Your will and way for my life, so that I will be ready to receive my blessing at the appointed time. In Jesus's name, amen.

Scriptures about Perseverance

> *I press toward the mark for the prize of the high calling of God in Christ Jesus.*

> *—Philippians 3:14*

> *Seek the Lord and his strength, seek his face continually.*

> *—1 Chronicles 16:11*

> *For ye have need of patience, that after ye have done the will of God, ye might receive the promise.*

> *—Hebrews 10:36*

Take the next two pages for your own personal study and devotional.

Personal Study and Devotional

Chapter 6

Personal Study and Devotional

Chapter 6

Chapter 7

No Condemnation

There is therefore now no condemnation to
them which are in Christ Jesus, who walk not
after the flesh, but after the Spirit.

—*Romans 8:1*

It does not matter if there was a fumble in the game, or
even a turnover. Remember, with God, you will always get
another chance to get it right. He loves you! He is cheer-
ing for you when no one else is. He is always encouraging
you. Sometimes you have to tune out the noise around
you and remain silent. Be still. He speaks to your heart, to
your spirit. Also, remember that God's children "hear His
voice, and He knows them," and a stranger will not "pluck
them out of His hand," according to John 10:27–28. He will
touch you even in your darkest moment.

Never continue to feel guilty for anything you may have
done wrong, whether intentionally or unintentionally. The

enemy loves to use guilt to get God's children to believe that God has not really forgiven them. That is a lie. You have already been forgiven. God is not like man; He will never hold something against you that you did wrong. He wants you to move on from it. Clean slate. When you move on from it, you free yourself.

If you do not, it's similar to having weights at your ankles that make it hard for you to take the ball down the field. Eventually, you will be tackled by the enemy. He wants your mind. If he can get that, he feels there is no turning back to God for help. He's got you. But, the devil is a liar! All you have to do is call on Jesus, and He will deliver you out of the hands of the enemy!

Remember to "think things that are good, lovely, and true," as Philippians 4:8 says. Release those chains. Release those weights. It's time to take the ball and run!

It doesn't matter what you did, you are forgiven. Keep going!

Meditate on this Scripture:

If we confess our sins, he is faithful and just to forgive us our sins, and to cleanse us from all unrighteousness.

—1 John 1:9

My Testimony

I had to realize that God wants me to be honest with Him. Totally and completely honest. I mean, He already knows what we've done anyway, right? LOL. But, truth, I began having heart-to-heart talks with the Lord in my twenties, after the relationship that helped cause my depression. I would tell Him how I felt about things and people. If I was struggling with something, I would tell Him about it and ask Him to help me. If I did something wrong, even intentionally, I would talk to Him about it afterward.

I like people keeping it real with me. Why wouldn't I keep it real with God? He created me, after all. He knows me. He knows if I will be interested in a guy. He knows if I will continue in an unequally yoked relationship. He knows if I will be tempted to do things I know I shouldn't do. He knows all, sees all, hears all.

I confessed. I felt guilty. I was low. I knew I hurt the one Who loved me most and was always there for me. He would never hurt me, even for the smaller sins—for example, telling a little white lie. It doesn't matter; sin is sin. The enemy tried to make me continue to feel bad, especially if my act was intentional. But I loved me too much to stay in a place of guilt. To love myself is what God wanted me to do. To dust myself off, pick myself up, and carry on with that day and the next, and the next. When I did that, I began to feel a little lighter. Soon, I forgot about whatever it was.

Remember, we only need to take that first step; God will take it from there. I say all this to remind everyone to release whatever it is God does not want you to hold on to, even if it is unforgiveness. Heal. Forgive. Continue in the things of God. Continue to do what you know is right. Remember, the Holy Spirit will lead you, "guide you into all truth," and teach you things you do not know, according to John 16:13.

I am reminded of Whitley Gilbert from the television series *A Different World*, but I will add on a word—LOL. Confess, relax, relate, release!

Amen.

A Prayer

Thank You, Lord, for forgiving me. There is nothing that is too hard for You to forgive. Thank You for Your Holy Spirit's leading me, guiding me, and teaching me when I don't know if something is right or wrong. Thank You for being a God of love and showing me how to grow in You. Help my hands to do what I have a hard time doing. I thank You, for my steps are ordered in Your Word. I know You want and have the best for me, and I want to stay in Your will and way. I thank You for the greater things that are coming! In Jesus's name, amen.

Scriptures to Help with Guilt

For all have sinned, and come short of the glory of God.

—*Romans 3:23*

Submit yourselves therefore to God. Resist the devil, and he will flee from you.

—James 4:7

Casting all your care upon him; for he careth for you.

—1 Peter 5:7

Fear not; for thou shall not be ashamed: neither be though confounded; for thou shalt not be put to shame: for thou shalt forget the shame of thy youth, and shalt not remember the reproach of thy widowhood anymore.

—Isaiah 54:4

As far as the east is from the west, [so] far hath he removed our transgressions from us.

—Psalms 103:12

Repent ye therefore, and be converted, that your sins may be blotted out, when the times of refreshing shall come from the presence of the Lord.

—Acts 3:19

Take the next two pages for your own personal study and devotional.

Personal Study and Devotional

Chapter 7

Personal Study and Devotional

Chapter 7

Chapter 8

An Intro to *The Green Light Series*

Now faith is the substance of things hoped for,
the evidence of things not seen.

—*Hebrews 11:1*

By now, you understand that no matter what you may have said or done, or how many times, God's grace is sufficient for you to recover from it. You must ask for His forgiveness and then forgive yourself, even for the things of the past. The next battle is going to be big for you...but you can do it with God's love and guidance! Smile.

What is it? It's called faith. You have to believe in things, promises, that you can't yet see! Faith begins with the letter *F*, which stands for *forward*. Wink. No matter how dim the view may appear, that's not really how it actually is...and God wants you to keep moving forward in faith!

The upcoming series, the *Green Light Series*, will begin with a guide to help you if you are going through a hard time in the area of faith. Before it comes out, I will leave you with a Scripture to meditate on and this to think about: After you take one step, God WILL Take you farther and farther! He only needs you to take the first step. Don't give up playing the game because you are closer to your pass completion than you think!! Smile.

Meditate on this Scripture:

I can do all things through Christ which strengtheneth me.

—*Philippians 4:13*

Personal Study and Devotional

Chapter 8

Personal Study and Devotional

Chapter 8